Dr. Roger L. Frye

and

Greg Solomon

Copyright © 2017 by Dr. Roger L. Frye / Greg Solomon

All rights reserved. No part of this publication may be reproduced, distributed or transmitted in any form or by any means, including photocopying, recording, or other electronic or mechanical methods, without the prior written permission of the publisher.

Unless otherwise noted, all Scripture quotations are taken from the New King James Version (NKJV). Copyright© 1979, 1980, 1982 by Thomas Nelson, Inc. Used by permission. All rights reserved.

Scripture quotations marked (ESV) are taken from the English Standard Version. Copyright© 2001, 2002, 2007 by Crossway Bibles. Used by permission.

Scripture quotations marked (CEV) are from the Contemporary English Version. Copyright© 1991, 1992, 1995 by American Bible Society. Used by permission.

Scripture quotations marked (NIV) are taken from the Holy Bible, New International Version. Copyright© 1973, 1978, 1984 by International Bible Society. Used by permission of Zondervan Bible Publishers.

Scriptures marked AMP are taken from the AMPLIFIED BIBLE (AMP): Scripture taken from the AMPLIFIED® BIBLE, Copyright © 1954, 1958, 1962, 1964, 1965, 1987 by the Lockman Foundation Used by Permission.

Scripture quotations in this publication are from THE MESSAGE. Copyright © by Eugene H. Peterson 1993, 1994, 1995, 1996, 2000, 2001, 2002. Used by permission of NavPress. All rights reserved. Represented by Tyndale House Publishers, Inc.

ISBN-13: 978-0-9790607-6-2

Financial Healing/Dr. Roger L. Frye/Greg Solomon — 1st ed.
10 9 8 7 6 5 4 3 2 1

Printed in the United States of America

Division of Human Improvement Specialists, llc.

www.hispubg.com | info@hispubg.com

Table Of Contents

CHAPTER ONE
The Need 5

CHAPTER TWO
Procedure for Cleansing and Blessing the Land 17

CHAPTER THREE
Procedure for Cleansing and Blessing the Home 27

CHAPTER FOUR
Appendices 37

    Appendix A. Prayers 37

    Appendix B. Mezuzah 45

    Appendix C. The Mandala and land defilement 48

    Appendix D. What to do if after having completed the cleansing and blessing exercises delineated in this book you still sense defilement or an evil presence 51

    Appendix E. Creating a Holy Atmosphere 52

    Appendix F. Communion Service to Cleanse the Land 55

    Appendix G. Some Uses of Salt in the Scriptures 60

    Appendix H. Trauma Bonds to Land 63

    Appendix I. Preparing the Anointing Oil 64

    Appendix J. Ley Lines 66

    Appendix K. Occultic Paraphernalia in the Home   by Greg Solomon 72

    Appendix L. Blessing Land 80

    Appendix M. Ungodly Portals 82

    Appendix N. Dream Catchers 82

Summary 85

CHAPTER ONE

The Need

Periodically we receive phone calls from people, frantic, because weird, poltergeist-type occurrences manifest in their home on a somewhat regular basis. They describe in a panicky voice the inexplicable phenomenon of noises in the attic, or an indoor plant sporadically moving violently like a tree in a wind storm, or a voice coming from another room. In these spooky cases I recommend we send a team to cleanse and bless the land and home. Usually the weirdness leaves immediately and the inhabitants experience the peace of God.

Typically, however, the occupants don't experience this type of creepiness and they don't perceive the need for land and home cleansing and blessing because the negative impact of the defilement appears much more subtly. Examples include couples facing a new tension in their relationship they had never experienced before moving into their new home; children waking up nightly screaming with terrifying nightmares even though they had never suffered such nightmares in the previous home; new diseases; sleeplessness; lack of peace, etc. Granted, natural causes may exist beneath these conditions and the first line of defense may lie in that direction. For example, the heightened illness could be the result of toxic mold in the home or living too close to a high-voltage power line and the tension in the marriage may be caused by the added strain to the budget due to buying a newer and larger home.

At the same time, please know that the spiritual dynamic represents another powerful, commonly occurring, underlying cause behind the above mentioned maladies. The land and home may be spiritually defiled and need cleansing and blessing. Even though the land and home don't particularly feel spiritually polluted to the home owner, it doesn't hurt to pray the prayers delineated in this book.

I'm glad my wife, Ruthie, and I (Roger) have prayed these prayers. When visitors come to our home (Frye's) we often receive compliments such as, "I really feel the peace of God in your home." Our goal in writing this book is that you will enjoy the same type of blessing in your home and land. Before beginning the process of praying all the prayers presented here I recommend that you read the book in its entirety, including the Appendices, so that you have a general idea and understanding of where you're headed. Don't merely use this book to gain head knowledge but treat it as a step-by-step manual to walk you through the process of cleansing and blessing your land and home.

What Can You Expect?

After conducting the land and home cleansing and blessing exercises delineated in this writing the owners or lessees often say that they feel lighter, like there is more joy and freedom in the atmosphere, that the heaviness is gone. I've had several people tell me that they feel like it's their home for the very first time—

that they feel at home in their home. Even if there is no known evidence to suggest that the land has been defiled, I recommend that every Christian family go through the following procedure. Sometimes we see dramatic results. For example, some couples report that the above mentioned marital tension and division lifted off their relationship after the land and home cleansing and blessing. Other people testify that their children are able to sleep in peace, free of the dreadful nightmares. Some individuals report an increase in physical health and vitality.

Farmers often testify that their crops do better and that they lose fewer livestock in the birthing process. One farmer testified that he had a portion of his 500 acres that was barren. Year after year he could get nothing to grow on that patch of farmland no matter what he tried. After cleansing and blessing the land, to his amazement, that barren patch of land yielded a plentiful harvest. Prayer ministers commonly hear these types of stories after the prayer team cleanses the land.

Most Christians seem to understand the importance of blessing their home but few understand the significance of cleansing and blessing the land. If the land has been defiled, just blessing the home doesn't solve any problems because the home rests on the land. If your house was built on defiled land you will continue to experience certain negative effects until you deal with the land issues. The Bible has a lot to say about the land and cleansing the land is the first place to start before blessing the home.

Why Does the Land Need Cleansing?

Certain sins exist that tend to defile the land. These sins may or may not have been committed by the present owners or tenants. In fact, people from many generations or centuries ago may be the ones responsible for defiling the property. Think of the land as you would a battery. It can store a negative charge as well as a positive. On the positive side, we know of certain places where believers feel the Presence of God in an unusually powerful way, where God seems to open the windows of heaven, where it's easy to pray and commune with the Lord. We know of such localities where Christians have gathered for many years to worship, pray, and minister the Word. One of these places is Moravian Falls in North Carolina where most believers effortlessly move into the "glory zone" as they worship God. Land can be influenced by the practices of people, either for good or for evil.

Another good example of this dynamic is found in the movie "War Room." There is a scene that depicts a retired pastor and his wife who are looking for a home to buy. The pastor walks into a closet and senses something stunning. He walks out with a big smile on his face and asks the realtor if that had been a prayer room. The realtor knew good and well that that was the very room where the owner, an elderly female prayer warrior, regularly met with God to do serious business in intercession. The pastor could sense it in his spirit because that constant activity of fervent prayer somehow mysteriously got imprinted on the walls, floor, and ceiling of that room.

Pathway to Freedom Ministries' goal in performing the land and home cleansing and blessing ministry is to first bring the

Christian's land and possessions up from negative numbers to zero. But just removing the negative, the evil influences, or the defilement is not enough. From zero we seek to move the land into the positive numbers. The legal possessors of the land can, by their righteous acts, the reading of Scripture out loud, by speaking blessings to the land, and by worshipping the Most High God, influence the land to move up to an even greater positive charge, so that when spiritually sensitive Christians step foot on the property they sense the peace, they feel the Presence of God.

Some scientists have concluded that inanimate objects record the sound of our voice and if that's true our words affect our home and land. The LORD said in Jeremiah 31:23 (ESV),

> *Thus says the LORD of hosts, the God of Israel:*
> *"Once more they shall use these words in the land of*
> *Judah and in its cities, when I restore their fortunes:*
> *'The LORD bless you, O habitation of righteousness,*
> *O holy hill!'"*

We need to speak forth God's praises on our land and we need to speak blessings over our land. When Jesus rode into Jerusalem on a colt the people cried out with a loud voice, "Blessed is the King who comes in the name of the Lord! Peace in heaven and glory in the highest!" And some of the Pharisees demanded that Jesus rebuke His disciples. He replied, "I tell you, if these were silent, the very stones would cry out" (Luke 19:40, ESV). Jesus knew that rocks were imprinted by the praises of His disciples.

We begin the land and home cleansing and blessing by dealing with the negative, the unrighteous deeds, the wickedness that led to the land's defilement. Simply put, defilement comes in through sin, not just through every petty sin, but through certain types of sin and sin patterns. Here are the sins that the Bible specifically declares pollute the land:

I. **SEXUAL SIN**

As the Holy Spirit inspired the Scriptures He interspersed a number of passages which speak about the defilement of land. For instance, in Leviticus 18:24-27 we read,

> *Do not defile yourselves with any of these things; for by all these the nations are defiled, which I am casting out before you. For **the land is defiled**; therefore I visit the punishment of its iniquity upon it, and the land vomits out its inhabitants. You shall therefore keep My statutes and My judgments, and shall not commit any of these abominations, either any of your own nation or any stranger who dwells among you (for all these abominations the men of the land have done, who were before you, and thus **the land is defiled**) (emphasis added).*

In the context of these verses He speaks of various forms of sexual sin, including adultery, incest, and bestiality. In short, sexual sin defiles the land. The prophet Jeremiah says it this way,

> *Lift up your eyes to the desolate heights and see: where have you not lain with men? By the road you*

*have sat for them like an Arabian in the wilderness; and **you have polluted the land** with your harlotries and your wickedness (Jeremiah 3:2, emphasis added).*

To say it succinctly, prostitution defiles the land. According to Dictionary.com the verb "defile" means, "to make foul, dirty, or unclean; pollute; taint; debase." In that same chapter Jeremiah says,

"So it came to pass, through her casual harlotry, that she defiled the land…(v.9a, emphasis added).

II. THE SHEDDING OF INNOCENT BLOOD

The shedding of innocent blood also defiles or pollutes the land. In Psalm 106:37-38 we read,

*They even sacrificed their sons and their daughters to demons, and shed innocent blood, the blood of their sons and daughters, whom they sacrificed to the idols of Canaan; and **the land was polluted with blood** (emphasis added).*

To "pollute" means essentially the same as to "defile." To pollute means "to make foul, unclean, or dirty."

Another example comes from the conflict between Cain and Abel. See what the Bible says in Genesis 4:8-12,

Now Cain talked with Abel his brother; and it came to pass, when they were in the field, that Cain rose up against Abel his brother and killed him. Then the LORD said to Cain, "Where is Abel your broth-

> er?" He said, "I do not know. Am I my brother's keeper?" And He said, "What have you done? The voice of your brother's blood cries out to Me from the ground. So now you are cursed from the earth, which has opened its mouth to receive your brother's blood from your hand. When you till the ground, it shall no longer yield its strength to you. A fugitive and a vagabond you shall be on the earth."

This curse on the land was severe because up until that time Cain made his living as a farmer. He depended on a good harvest to support himself and his family. After God cursed the land Scripture doesn't say anything about Cain farming again. The Bible doesn't clarify it but perhaps it became so difficult to grow decent crops that he gave up the trade. It does, however, say that he went on to build cities. Cain may have had to give up farming but after we cleanse and bless the land it is common to hear testimonies of greatly improved harvests.

III. Broken Covenants

Broken covenants also defile the land.

> Now there was a famine in the days of David for three years, year after year; and David inquired of the Lord. And the Lord answered, "It is because of Saul and his
> bloodthirsty house, because he killed the Gibeonites."
> (2 Samuel 21:1).

King Saul had killed some Gibeonites, violating the covenant that Israel's earlier leader, Joshua, had made with them. As a consequence the land became defiled and would not produce the necessary crops. After David dealt with the situation and brought restitution it says,

> *So they performed all that the king commanded. And after that God heeded the prayer for the land.*

An example of a broken covenant is unfaithfulness to one's spouse. Marriage is a covenant relationship and broken marriage covenants defile the land so that subsequent married couples moving on that defiled land often face added marital stress.

IV.   THE WORSHIP OF FALSE GODS AND GODDESSES

Idol worship or the worship of false gods also defiles the land. In Ezekiel 38:18 we read,

> *Therefore I poured out My fury on them for the blood they had shed on **the land**, and for their idols with which they had **defiled it** (emphasis added).*

I include witchcraft and satanic activities under this category. In one sense an idol is anything we look to for security or self-worth other than Jesus such as money, a large retirement account, a large home, a high-paying job, etc. But I'm not sure if these kinds of idols represent the type of idolatry that defiles the land. I believe that the idolatry that defiles the land is the kind that includes the overt veneration of statues of gods or goddesses, witchcraft ceremonies and practices, satanic rituals, and the worship of deities other than the Most High God, Yahweh.

Because of these four classes of sins the land becomes wounded and needs healing. The Lord says this regarding the responsibility of His people and the benefits that follow obedience:

> *If My people who are called by My name will humble themselves, and pray and seek My face, and turn from their wicked ways, then I will hear from heaven, and will forgive their sin and* **heal their land** *(2 Chronicles 7:14, emphasis added).*

According to the Word of God the Israelites' land needed healing. And if it needed healing it was because the land was wounded. In Isaiah 55:12 we read (ESV),

> *For you shall go out in joy and be led forth in peace; the mountains and the hills before you shall break forth into singing, and all the trees of the field shall clap their hands.*

According to this passage, the land becomes influenced by our emotions, both positive and negative. On the negative side, the land absorbs the shock, trauma, fear, terror, pain, hopelessness, angst, etc., associated with humans' traumatic events. After dealing with the sins and iniquities defiling the land, then we need to ask God to heal the land. Ask Him to pull up the trauma and associated emotions from the land.

Evil spirits take advantage of the sins committed on the land and the trauma inflicted on the inhabitants and these demons bring defilement to the land at a deeper level. They aim to defile the inhabitants that live on the polluted land, seeking to draw them into sin and make their lives miserable. Once the owner or tenant deals with the sin issues through confession and renunciation, the evil spirits must be expelled from the property.

Keep in mind that God places a higher value on the land than most Christians realize. For example, in Leviticus 25:23-24 we read,

> *The land shall not be sold permanently, for the land is Mine; for you are strangers and sojourners with Me. And in all the land of your possession you shall grant redemption of the land.*

These verses speak specifically of the land of Palestine. He divided it once for all time in the days of Joshua among the twelve tribes of Israel and their clans. Every 50 years He required that the land had to go back to that original division. The land of the Israelites was not to be sold permanently. Provision was made for property to be sold in case of necessity, but only temporarily. It was to return to the original owner, or his heirs, in the year of Jubilee or every 50 years. We're not under the Mosaic ritual law as New Testament saints but I mention this law to underscore the fact that God says a lot about the land and places great importance on it. Therefore, it behooves the believer to likewise treat the land as a wise steward of God's possession.

A Prayer of Surrender

The un-surrendered heart presents the first major obstacle in experiencing the lasting peace of Jesus Christ in your home. A prayer team can be called in to rid the home and land of any defilement and positive effects are enjoyed immediately. However, if those in authority in the home refuse to bow their heart and knee to the Lord Jesus Christ they will be unable to effectively resist the enemy's attacks to wreck havoc and disturb the peace.

Please pray the following suggested prayer and do your best to pray it from your heart:

> *Lord Jesus Christ of Nazareth, I thank You for giving me the gift of life. I acknowledge that You have given me a free will so that I can either choose You or reject You. Thank You for Your love for me that never gives up. Thank You that You died for me in order to free me from Satan's slavery and give me eternal life. Thank You that You rose again from the grave. Thank You that You want to have intimate fellowship with me. Forgive me for the times I have gone my own way, the times I have resisted Your will for my life, for making major decisions without consulting You. I confess my sin of passivity toward You, for not seeking You with all my heart, for not trusting You with my life. Today, I give You my heart Lord Jesus. I surrender all that I am to You. I give You my past, present, and future and I choose to trust You. Lord, I abandon myself to You and I ask You to fill me with the Holy Spirit to enable me to live the victorious Christian life. I declare that Jesus Christ is my Lord. Amen*

CHAPTER TWO

Procedure for Cleansing and Blessing the Land

Meet outside in a central location on the property and put on the armor of God as outlined in Ephesians.

I. **Prayers to Cleanse the Land.**

The owners and team members take turns praying the following prayers:

1. *Heavenly Father, we ask You to cleanse this land from every blasphemous activity, all worship of false gods and goddesses, and the sin of indifference to You. Cleanse the land of every activity that was inspired by Satan in an attempt to diminish Your glory.*

2. *Almighty God, we also reject and renounce all the sins people committed against each other on this land. Let every act of violence and sexual violation be cleansed by the blood of Jesus Christ of Nazareth. Righteous Judge*

of the Universe, we ask that You would annul all ungodly covenants and break all agreements with Sheol made on this land according to Isaiah 28:18. We reject and renounce those covenants and agreements and ask You to cleanse this land of their impact. Where ungodly covenants were formed, You released a curse against the land. We admit that it was right, just, and appropriate for You to release those curses upon this land but we ask that they be broken and sent to the Cross of Calvary.

3. *We ask You, Most High God, to destroy the power of every method used to confirm and seal these ungodly covenants such as words, blood sacrifices, fire, written pacts, sexual activities, ceremonies, symbols, clothes, titles, colors, sounds, numbers, fragrances and all other tools. We ask You to put all of this under the blood of Christ so that these mechanisms have no impact at all on this land.*

4. *Heavenly Father, we come to You today, renouncing the sins which people have committed against each other on this land. Please identify every activity or sin of the heart committed on this land from the beginning of the world. We ask You to bring every sin of commission or omission under the blood of Jesus Christ and purge this land from the defilement of every evil activity, negative words and mindsets.*

5. *Almighty God, we reject and renounce and bring to You all of the violence that people have done on this*

land. We ask that You bring under the blood all acts of violence such as war, pillaging, murder, abortion, suicide, child abuse, spousal abuse, elder abuse, worker abuse, torture, human sacrifice, rape, and torture of animals. We recognize that the land is deeply stained by violence that is carried out on it.

However, we also know that the appalling violence done against Jesus Christ on the cross broke the power of the enemy and all that he defiled. Jesus' life, death and resurrection made available the power to cleanse and sanctify any and all polluted land. So we implore You to remove all of the judgments against this land that came as a result of these sins of violence. We ask that the structures and devices allowed by the violence that empowered the enemy, would be destroyed. We ask that You would alleviate all the grief and distress on this land. We ask You Father to send Your holy angels to clean up any blood that was spilled on this land through acts of violence and take that blood to the place You want it to be. Please release Your angels to clean up every particle of that blood down to the atomic and subatomic level, in Jesus' Name.

6. *Most High God, You made people to be good stewards of the land You created. We confess that mankind has often refused to care for the land and to exploit it for their selfish purposes and we agree with You that this is sin. Forgive mankind for neglecting to care for the land as You originally designed and for not walking in*

our God-ordained stewardship of the land. We acknowledge that the land belongs to You and so often mankind treats the land as a personal possession to be used selfishly.

7. *Father, we ask You to cleanse this land of all the defilement brought by any animal that killed a person on this property (Genesis 9:5).*

8. *We ask You Father to cleanse this land of all worship of ancestors. We declare that worship belongs only to the Creator of the ends of the earth, the One Triune God: Father, Son, and Holy Spirit.*

9. *We purify with the blood of Jesus Christ the air, water, ground, fire, and the forces of nature and claim them for the Most High God's holy use. We ask You Father to cut off anything coming against the inhabitants of this land from the underworld and close any portals of access there, in Jesus' Name. We ask You LORD to cut off anything coming against the inhabitants of this land from the second heaven and close any portals of access there. We ask you Father to bind the evil spirit world from any access routes to or from this place, in Jesus' Name.*

II. **Communion (See appendix F for a suggested communion service)**

After giving thanks and asking God to bless the bread and juice, partake of the communion[i] elements. Dig a hole for the fruit of the vine and the bread left over from communion. Place the remaining portion of the bread in the hole. Pour a large portion of the fruit of the vine over the bread. Cover the elements with dirt. When you are finished, make this declaration as a group in unison:

> *By the authority of the Name of Jesus and by His shed blood and broken body, we reclaim and redeem this land. We declare that by the Spirit of God, it is holy ground, sanctified and cleansed, set apart for the glory of God, and Him alone.*

Create a canopy of praise to God by singing a chorus. Worship Him, and you will prepare an atmosphere for His Spirit to come and open a lasting portal to His presence.

> *Lord, lift up a canopy of praise over this property, in Jesus' Name.*

III. Sprinkling of Salt (See Appendix G for information about the use of salt)

A team member sprinkles small amounts of blessed salt onto the land.

As the land is being salted the team member says,

> *In Jesus' Name I declare that this land is healed and there will be no death or barrenness upon it.*

IV. Declaration

The owners join hands and pray this prayer in unison if both spouses are present:

> *Heavenly Father, we thank You that we have been*

purchased by the precious blood of Jesus Christ of Nazareth. And because we have been purchased by His blood, we are children of God. As His children, we live in Jesus and He lives in us. And because He lives in us we have the right to prevail against the enemy because He prevailed. Now as victors, we break every evil curse, spell, hex or demonic assignment that has come onto our land and our home. We send these curses, spells, hexes and assignments to the Cross of Christ and command them to be halted at the Cross of Calvary. We declare that their power over our land is broken, in Jesus' Name.

We receive every blessing that You, heavenly Father, have for us. We take back any ground that was ever given to any demonic spirit on this property, whether it was given knowingly or unknowingly. We renounce all occultic or satanic activity performed on this land. We cut all ungodly ties with any previous owners or possessors of this land and home. We declare that no evil spirit has any right to this land and home, in Jesus' Name. We declare them defeated and they have no rights to our home and land. By the authority Christ has given us we command all evil spirits to leave this land and never return. Every evil spirit is defeated because of the finished work of Jesus on Calvary's cross and His resurrection, so you cannot stay. Leave now, in Jesus' Name.

V.   Staking the Land

Before the cleansing ceremony takes place, make ready four stakes that can be easily driven into the land. They should be four to five inches in length. Places like The Home Depot sell precut stakes that have a nice point on one end. They are a little too long to easily drive them all the way into the ground so you need to saw them in half. With a Sharpie pen write a Scripture verse on each stake. My favorite verse in this case is Joshua 24:15 which reads,

> *As for me and my house we will serve the Lord,*

Or you may use other verses that fit the situation.

1. Stand together as the head of the household makes this declaration before you drive the first stake into the corner of your property.

   Heavenly Father, I agree with You that the sins of violence, the worshipping of false gods and goddesses, sex outside of marriage, perverted sex, incest, broken covenants, and the cutting of ungodly covenants that have taken place on this land and property are wicked, ungodly, and against You. I utterly reject and renounce these sins. I ask You to remove every spirit of infirmity, bondage, fear, divination, harlotry, deep sleep, ill will, haughtiness, perverseness, anti-Christ, deaf and dumbness, heaviness, lying, jealousy, stupor, and error that has come to this land and property from the beginning of the world. I ask You to break all demonic assignments and curses that have come

> as a result of these sins and patterns of iniquity. I ask You to sever all ungodly soul ties between every prior owner, occupant, trespasser, claimant, tenant and me and my household. I ask You to break any trauma bonds anyone has to this land. Release them from this land and release this land from them, in Jesus' Name, Amen.

(See Appendix H for information about trauma bonds)

> I take my authority as the legal owner (or tenant) of this property. I set new boundary lines by the Spirit of God and say to all demonic forces that they will not cross, trespass, or project onto this land, property and home. They will not bring in hexes, vexes, spells, incantations, evil spirits or assignments against me, or my household, land, property, possessions, pets or other animals. Father, cleanse this land by the blood of Jesus. Create new boundaries. I reclaim and set apart this home, land and property for Yahweh's use and His alone, in Jesus' Name, Amen.

2. Take the first stake, anoint it with blessed oil and drive it into a corner of your property at the legal boundary line. It's better to drive the stake a few inches inside your property line than it is to place it over the line. You don't have the spiritual authority to cleanse your neighbor's property, unless granted, and your efforts will not produce the desired results. If your property line butts up against government property you may not have to be so careful because you have some authority to cleanse that land. You

have a measure of authority there because, as a citizen and tax payer, you are part owner. But it is always best to stay within the recognized legal boundary of your land. Pour some anointing oil over the stake and around the corner area of the boundary line. (See Appendix I for information about anointing oil)

3. Dribble anointing oil on the ground near the property line as you make your way to the next corner proceeding in a clockwise manner. As the anointing oil is being applied, make faith declarations such as,

> *All evil must leave this land, in Jesus' Name; I declare that this land belongs to the Lord Jesus Christ; Most High God, let Your glory rest upon this land; and Let Your peace be upon this land.*

Do the same at each corner of your land until you have placed one stake at each of the four corners. As you walk the property boundaries discern the presence of an ungodly ley line (See Appendix J for information on ley lines). If you sense one exists take the necessary steps to cleanse it and pray,

> *Heavenly Father, please cleanse the ley lines attached to this property.*

4. Bless the land. Gather as a team and say in unison several times,

> *The Lord bless this land.*

I encourage the owner or tenant to speak blessings over the land on a regular basis (See Appendix A for suggested prayers).

CHAPTER THREE

Procedure for Cleansing and Blessing the Home

I. Prayer of Dedication

Pick a central place in your home, join hands and have the head of the household or the person in authority in the home make this dedication:

> *Most High God and loving Heavenly Father, I declare that You are the Lord of my life and the Lord of this home. I have chosen to make You my fortress, my strength, and my ever present help in times of trouble. Now I ask You, in the Name of Jesus and by the power of the Holy Spirit, to come and receive my home and all that I own. I give them to You. I ask You to bring to the light and help us to see any hidden thing that has brought wickedness, a disruption of peace, nightmares, disunity, evil spirits or an unholy frame of mind into my home, land, possessions and pets. Lord Jesus, I ask You to break the power of the enemy in every room of this home, on every possession and object, on my animals, and on every portion of my land and property. Lord Jesus, remove all evil from this place. Lord, fill my*

home with Your presence and use it for Your purposes. Set it apart for Your use alone and loose Your holy angels to guard the doors and provide a shield to protect all that You have given me. Protect this home from all evil, division, disharmony, sickness, disease and destruction of every kind. I declare that this home, land, property, and all my possessions and pets belong to the Triune God, Father, Son and Holy Spirit. I am simply a steward overseeing everything You have placed within my hands. As for me and my family we will serve You alone. You are my refuge and strength and I turn to You at all times. I trust in You and evil has no place here. You are my deliverer and I declare that Jesus Christ, the Holy One of Israel, is Lord of my home. Thank You, Lord, in Jesus' Name, Amen.

II. Prayers over Each Area of the Home

1. The Front Door — Threshold

The head of the household prays:

Lord Jesus, I present this land, property, home and all the inhabitants of this household, with its possessions, to You. Now come and break and remove every hex, vex, spell, evil spirit and assignment of the kingdom of darkness from this home. Remove every spirit of infirmity, fear, divination, harlotry, bondage, haughtiness, perverseness, deaf and dumbness, heaviness, lying, anti-Christ, stupor, ill will, deep sleep, error and jealousy by the power and authority of Your blood and Your Name. Place a hedge of thorns and a wall of protection around this home. Bless our family with Your peace, protection and prosperity. May the favor of the LORD rest upon us. Thank You, Lord, for Your blessing and presence in this house, in Jesus' Name. Amen.

A team member sprinkles a very small amount of salt on the floor and another team member anoints the doorways and windows with oil in each room while saying something such as,

I command all evil to leave this room, in Jesus' Name. I bless this room and speak the peace of Jesus Christ over this area.

2. The Formal Dining Room

Team members and/or family members may take turns praying the following prayers. If any team members discern demonic points of contact or the presence of any evil entity in areas of the home, deal with them decisively by commanding them to leave.

Father in Heaven, break any and all assignments of the kingdom of darkness on this room and the items here. Cleanse and sanctify them for Your holy use. Assemble people around this table for warm fellowship and encouragement. Let the interactions that transpire here bring camaraderie, unity, healing and comfort to all who meet here. May they bring glory to Your Name, in Jesus' Name, Amen.

3. **The Kitchen and Breakfast Dining Area**

   Father in Heaven, break any and all assignments of the kingdom of darkness on the room and the items here. Sanctify and cleanse them for Your holy use. Keep all anger, strife, unforgiveness and division from this room where the family members come every day for physical nourishment. Let Your manifest presence and Your peace rest upon this room. Almighty God, remove every spirit of fear, depression, hopelessness, despair, and anger from this place. Remove every impediment to the blessings You have for this family. May the individuals who gather here remember that You alone are our provider no matter what the circumstances. We ask for Your blessing upon this family according to Your Word. Release Your blessing upon the pantry and the cupboards so that they will always be full and bless this family to always have a willing and obedient heart to share with others, in Jesus' Name, Amen.

4. **The Living Room or Den**

   Father in Heaven, break any assignments of the kingdom of darkness on this room and the items here. Sanctify and cleanse them for Your holy use. Keep all anger, strife, and division from this room. Help the family members relax and enjoy their time with each other and with their friends. Close any portals of access to Satan's evil kingdom (See Appendix M). Enable the family to guard what they see with their eyes, hear with their ears, and say with their mouths. Hide this family from the enemy as they meet in this room and let Your peace, joy, and love abide in this place, in Jesus' Name, Amen.

5. The Study, Office, or Library

    Heavenly Father, break any all assignments of the kingdom of darkness on this room and the possessions here. Sanctify and cleanse them for Your holy use. Teach this family where true wisdom and understanding is to be found and keep them from trusting in human wisdom above trusting in Your Word. Reveal Yourself as the God of truth, the All-knowing Creator of the Universe who sees all things. Without You, O' Lord, we go about in ignorance so teach us to seek You, in Jesus' Name, Amen.

6. The Master Bedroom

The husband and wife pray this prayer in unison if both spouses are present:

Father in Heaven, break and remove any and all assignments of the kingdom of darkness on this room and the possessions here. Sanctify and cleanse them for Your holy use. Keep all anger, strife, and division from this room. Help us to remember to reconcile every difference between us before we sleep each night so that we give the enemy no place in our lives and relationship. Remove all influence of any evil entity in this place. We decree and declare that all the furni-

ture in this room is set apart, sanctified, and holy unto You, O' God. Bless our marriage and increase our love. Strengthen our communication, and cause our intimacy level to increase as the years go by. Let Your manifest Presence abide in this room, in Jesus' Name, Amen.

7. The Bedrooms—Infant, Child, Young Adult

   Father in Heaven, break, shatter, dissolve and destroy any and all assignments of the kingdom of darkness on this room and the possessions here. Sanctify and cleanse them for Your holy purposes. Keep all loneliness, depression, fear, false guilt, condemnation, shame, and valuelessness from anyone who sleeps in this room. Remove and destroy every assignment against their destiny. Seal this room with Your presence and peace, in Jesus' Name, Amen.

8. The Guestroom

   Father in Heaven, break, shatter, dissolve and destroy all assignments of the kingdom of darkness on this room and the objects here. Sanctify and cleanse them for Your holy use. Remove and cut off every spirit of infirmity, bondage, fear, deep sleep, divination, harlotry, haughtiness, perverseness, ill will, anti-Christ, deaf and dumbness, heaviness, lying, jealousy, stupor, and error. Let Your manifest Presence abide in the room. Bless this room and may Your peace permeate the atmosphere so that the guests may rest in Your love, in Jesus' Name, Amen.

9. The Bathrooms

Father in Heaven, break, shatter, dissolve, and destroy any and all assignments of the kingdom of darkness on this room and the possessions here. Sanctify and cleanse them for Your holy use. Remove every spirit of harlotry from this place. Remove all spirits of condemnation, lies, valuelessness, and vain imaginations. Remove all lies against one's sense of value and true identity. Close any ungodly portals. Holy Spirit, fill this room with Your Presence and Your power and bring Your peace to this room, in Jesus' Name, Amen.

10. The Hallways

Heavenly Father, break, shatter, dissolve, and destroy any and all assignments of the kingdom of darkness on this hallway. Sanctify and cleanse this hallway for Your holy use. Remove any evil entity or demonic device that was placed here to keep the family disconnected to each other emotionally and spiritually. Please help us establish healthy boundaries, while at the same time, enjoying unity and appropriate levels of intimacy. Lord bring Your peace to this area of the home, in Jesus' Name, Amen.

11. The Staircases

Heavenly Father, break, shatter, dissolve, and destroy any and all assignments of the kingdom of darkness on this staircase. Sanctify and cleanse this staircase for Your holy use. I command any and all evil spirits assigned to this staircase to leave now and never return. You will not cause injury or mishaps to any of the occupants or guests while ascending or descending these steps, in Jesus' Name. Most High God, I ask for Your protection on all who use these stairs and I thank You for it, in Jesus' Name, Amen.

12. The Closets

Sprinkle a small amount of salt in each closet and pray:

I command all evil to leave this room, in Jesus' Name. I bless this room and speak the peace of Jesus Christ over this area.

13. The Game Room/Media Room

Make sure to rid the room of any demonic games, demonized record albums, witchcraft books, pornography, ungodly movies, and movies that present witchcraft in a positive light. The husband and wife must be in agreement.

Father in Heaven, break, shatter, dissolve, and destroy any and all assignments of the kingdom of darkness on this room and the possessions here. Sanctify and cleanse them for Your holy use. I command any demonic spirits to leave this room and never return, in Jesus' Name. I bless this room and speak the peace of Jesus Christ over this area.

14. The Laundry Room

Sprinkle a small amount of salt in the laundry room and pray:

I command all evil to leave this room, in Jesus' Name. I bless this room and speak the peace of Jesus Christ over this area.

15. The Basement

Father in Heaven, break, shatter, dissolve, and destroy any and all assignments of the kingdom of darkness on this room and the possessions here. Sanctify and cleanse them for Your holy use. Cut off anything coming from the Netherworld against this family and close any portals of access, in Jesus' Name, Amen.

16. The Garage

Anoint the doorway coming in and going out and the garage door itself. Also anoint the vehicles and pray this prayer.

Father in Heaven, I present this garage and entry to my home to You. Break, shatter, dissolve, and destroy every hex, vex, spell, evil spirit and assignment of the kingdom of darkness on this place. Remove every spirit of infirmity, fear, divination, harlotry, bondage, haughtiness, perverseness, deaf and dumbness, ill will, deep sleep, heaviness, lying, anti-Christ, stupor, error and jealousy from entering this place. I decree and declare that Jesus Christ of Nazareth is Lord of this area of this home. Lord, may Your holy angels keep guard to protect this home from the onslaught of the enemy. I thank You Lord that You are our shield and protector, in Jesus' Mighty Name, Amen.

17. The Attic or Storage Room

Heavenly Father, break, shatter, dissolve, and destroy any and all assignments of the kingdom of darkness on this area of the home. Drive far from this place all the snares of the enemy and keep them from returning. We bless this area and ask for a protective hedge of thorns around this place, in Jesus' Name, Amen.

18. The Terrace, Deck, Porch, or Garden

Lord Jesus, in many incidences You withdrew with Your friends for silence and refreshment. In like manner we ask You to be present with Your children in this place so that they can enjoy good fellowship, rest, and relaxation. Make it a place of peace and serenity, in Jesus' Name, Amen.

CHAPTER FOUR

APPENDICES

APPENDIX A. PRAYERS

Here are some additional prayers to pray over your land and home that you may find to be a huge help in maintaining God's protection and peace in your life and in the lives of those who dwell in your home. I personally pray the first two prayers on a daily basis but the Holy Spirit may lead you differently.

A Prayer to Pray Regularly in Your Home

Praise and worship be to The Most High God, the God of all created beings. For by Him; the salvation, and the power, and the Kingdom of our God and the authority of His Christ have come. Hallelujah! The evil deceiver has been defeated because of the Blood of the Lamb.

As a Christian, I now give testimony to the authority of the Lord Jesus Christ, the Holy One of Israel over my home and property located at _____. I ask You

Father to loose with Jesus' Blood, the wicked spiritual forces of evil including all rulers, authorities and cosmic powers of this dark age who are not of the Lord Jesus Christ as He sees and numbers them in this place.

By the power of Jesus Christ of Nazareth, all forces of evil within this home and land, are now bound from any and all communication, interplay or interaction between themselves or any other forces of evil. Any and all evil access routes, to or from this home and land, are now severed as I purify with the Blood of the Lamb the AIR, WATER, GROUND, FIRE, and the FORCES OF NATURE and claim them for Christ Jesus anew and consecrate them unto Him.

I ask you Father to cut off anything coming against us from the second heaven and close any portals of access there and I ask You Father to cut off any evil forces coming against us from the Netherworld by the Blood, the Cross and the Name of Jesus and close any portals of access there. I take authority over and send back anything coming from the spirit world against any member of my immediate family and our properties. I now repel and utterly defeat any attack launched against us.

In the name of Jesus, I now bind any darkness brought into this home by us or anybody else that has been in this home. Such darkness is now rendered utterly powerless by the Blood of Jesus Christ, the Light of the world, and cannot communicate, interact or interplay with themselves or any other evil forces. Nor can they influence, harm or inhibit us today.

I now seal this home and land by the Blood of the Lamb shed on the cross of Calvary. I invite with thanksgiving, the full and manifest presence of the Holy Spirit of Yahweh to come and dwell here with all wisdom and knowledge for the glory of Almighty God through His Son Jesus Christ, the Holy One of Israel.

I take authority over every hex, vex, spell, curse, gossip, psychic-soulish prayer, hoodoo, voodoo, Satanism, Santeria, negative confession, Muslim prayers, Freemasonry curses and prayers, witchcraft and all such things used against me, my wife/husband (name), children _____ (name(s), and grandchildren (name them if applicable). In Jesus' Name, I break the power of those negative words and cast them down to the ground. Any demons assigned to us through those words and ungodly activities I now assign to dry places. I condemn every tongue that has risen up against us in judgment, according to Isaiah 54:17. I cut off any witch or warlock who is cursing us from accessing future powers of darkness and I ask you to save and bless the witch or warlock, in Jesus' Name.

I lift up a canopy of praise over us today. I submit totally unto Your will, Most High God, and praise You for Your manifest presence and Your protection of Your children here today, in Jesus' mighty Name and for His sake. (Adapted from One Accord Ministries, adapted by Roger Frye)

ANOTHER PRAYER TO PRAY OVER YOUR FAMILY

In Jesus' Name I declare the victory of the cross and the resurrection over me, spouse (name), children (name(s), and grandchildren (names, if applicable). I declare Deuteronomy 29:29 over my children and grandchildren. The secret things belong to the LORD our God, but those things which are revealed belong to us and to our children forever, that we may do all the words of this law. Come Your Kingdom, be done Your will on earth as it is in heaven in _____ (name immediate family members). I bless myself, and _____ (name family members) with seeing eyes, hearing ears, and a heart to know and understand the truth of God. I speak the peace of Jesus Christ over my family. I speak peace over this home and I ask You Lord to enthrone Jesus on this land, Amen.

A PRAYER OF CONSECRATION TO PRAY OVER YOUR HOME

I consecrate my home today to the Holy Spirit. I consecrate the words spoken between all who dwell here and I bless our willingness to truly listen to and understand each other. I bless our willingness and ability to respect and honor each other's boundaries and needs. I bless our willingness and ability to express love to each other by honoring one another's love languages. I bring this home under the rule of Jesus Christ and under the filling of the Holy Spirit, in Jesus' Name, Amen.

A Prayer of Repentance for Misuse of Land

Paul declared in Romans 8:19-22,

> *For the earnest expectation of the creation eagerly waits for the revealing of the sons of God. For the creation was subjected to futility, not willingly, but because of Him who subjected it in hope; because the creation itself also will be delivered from the bondage of corruption into the glorious liberty of the children of God. For we know that the whole creation groans and labors with birth pangs together until now.*

Because of the sins of mankind all creation groans. This problem will be resolved with the revealing of the sons of God. In the meantime there are some things we can do to restore the land.

One misuse of land that you may have never considered is the failure to observe the Sabbath rest. God Himself rested on the seventh day and He commanded the Children of Israel to not only rest every seventh day but to let the land rest every seventh year. It was to remain at rest with no seeds planted and crops harvested. Violation of this clear command brought dire consequences as the Children of Israel went into exile for 70 years - one year for every Sabbath year they violated.

It has been proven scientifically that all of us have ancestors that participated in the sin against the land in Canaan. That sin gets in the bloodline and is passed down through what is called iniquity. To take away Satan's legal rights we recommend that you pray the following prayer.

> *"Heavenly Father, I confess and renounce my sin and the sins of my ancestors for not giving the land a Sab-*

bath rest. In not giving the land a Sabbath rest we rejected Your principles and ordinances. We went our own way and did what was right in our own eyes. Lord, please break off all the consequences on me and upon the land for not honoring Your requirements. Almighty God, I confess and repent for all those in my generations past, all the way back to Adam and Eve, who, because of their sin, released thorns and thistles into the ground placing a curse on the produce of the land. Lord, I confess and renounce the sin in my family line of turning to fertility cults and sacrificing to other gods as a way to bring blessings upon the land. I confess and renounce the sin in my generational line of all ungodly dependence on the land. I confess and renounce the sin of worshipping the land. I break all ungodly ties for me and my ancestors with the land. I ask You Lord to break all blood ties that me, my family, or others have to my property, in Jesus' Name, Amen."

LAND REPENTANCE PRAYER BY PAUL COX
www.aslansplace.com

"Lord, I come before you on behalf of my family line and myself in regard to all of the issues that have cursed or otherwise tainted our land.

Lord, I repent and renounce for:

- Those who dedicated land to the works of freemasonry, religion, ungodly organizations or Satanism
- Knowingly or unknowingly bringing curses on the

land through sacrifices or rituals
- Husbands and wives that were not in unity about their land
- Wives that tilled the land thinking it was dedicated to God, but it was not
- Those whose hands were defiled because they tilled the land until it became fruitless
- Women that reaped the consequences of a bent back because of tilling ungodly land; thinking they were doing a righteous thing, but actually taking on burdens their husband should have carried; resulting in empty works because the land was dedicated for ungodly purposes
- Husbands that would not till their land and let their wives do it, bringing disunity to the family
- Husbands that traded the land and went against Godly principles for tiling the land
- Those that purchased land and allowed defilement to come upon it through ungodly agreements with unrighteous authorities, especially their city of residence
- Going to places in the city for meetings that may have been dedicated to ungodly purposes, thus bringing home defilement on our feet that allowed evil hitchhikers to accompany us
- Letting any secret tunnels or underground networks to be attached to our property, or allowing unrighteous access through water rights or ungodly waterways

Lord, please disconnect our elemental inheritance, especially any water or mineral rights, on our land from all ungodly governmental authorities.

I repent and renounce for any who took our properties' resources and squandered them away, or used them in an ungodly way. Lord, please protect our resources from any ungodly governmental authorities.

I renounce ungodly governmental authorities that mapped out our property's location and tracked it in order to pursue ownership, or to steal our inheritance or the resources on the land. Lord, please remove our property from the enemy's radar.

I repent and renounce for those that connected to a death spirit through suicidal thoughts and/or hopelessness, valuing property and finances more than life; and for those that committed suicide on land, enabling a curse of death. Lord, please disconnect my land from all spirits of death and suicide.

I repent and renounce for:

- *Those of freemasonry that built the aqueduct, as well as any rituals or sacrifices that took place during the building*
- *Those that ran into the city before it was a city in an effort to control all the resources of that land*
- *Those that stole land from the Native Americans and for all resulting bloodshed*

Lord, please disconnect our land from the blood that

cries out and from any relics that could have been buried on our land before we owned it."

Appendix B. Mezuzah

Something else you might want to think about and pray about is the Mezuzah. I don't believe in using lucky charms to protect your home but the concept of the mezuzah comes from God Himself where He said,

> *Hear, O Israel: The LORD our God, the LORD is one!⁵ You shall love the LORD your God with all your heart, with all your soul, and with all your strength. ⁶ "And these words which I command you today shall be in your heart. ⁷ You shall teach them diligently to your children, and shall talk of them when you sit in your house, when you walk by the way, when you lie down, and when you rise up. ⁸ You shall bind them as a sign on your hand, and they shall be as frontlets between your eyes. ⁹ You shall write them on the doorposts of your house and on your gates (Deuteronomy 6:4-9).*

I know that we as Christians are not under the Mosaic ritual law so I believe its use is optional and that you should be led by the Holy Spirit.

The mezuzah contains, in a decorative case usually, a piece of parchment with Hebrew words of the first paragraphs of Deuteronomy 6:4-9 and Deuteronomy 11:13-21. These passages make up the Jewish prayer which is called the Shema Yisrael.

The mezuzah is attached to the doorframe in obedience to the Biblical command. The mezuzah is a constant reminder and public proclamation that the LORD delivers his people. It calls us to remember the exodus from Egyptian slavery, when the blood of the lamb was applied on the doorpost to identify the Jewish homes that God passed over during the last plague, the death of the first born.

Every mezuzah has on its face the Hebrew letter "shin" which resembles the "W" in the English alphabet. The shin is found in a lot of significant Hebrew words. For example, one of the names of God is "El Shaddai" which means "Almighty God, the All Sufficient One." And the first letter of the word "Shaddai" is the shin. "Shaddai" also serves as an acronym for *Shomer Daltot Yisrael*, "Guardian of Israel's doors."

Jews affix the mezuzah outside the house on the doorpost of the main entry, on the right side as you're going in. Customarily the Jewish people kiss the mezuzah before leaving the house and before entering the house. The mezuzah stands for "El Shaddai protect the family." In the old classic movie "Ben Hur" you see him kissing the mezuzah when he came home after his ordeal of serving as a slave and being adopted as a son of a powerful Roman senator. The mezuzah and the shin on the doorpost communicate the idea of God's protection.

Some pictures of the mezuzah are shown on the next two pages.

LAND AND HOME CLEANSING AND BLESSING

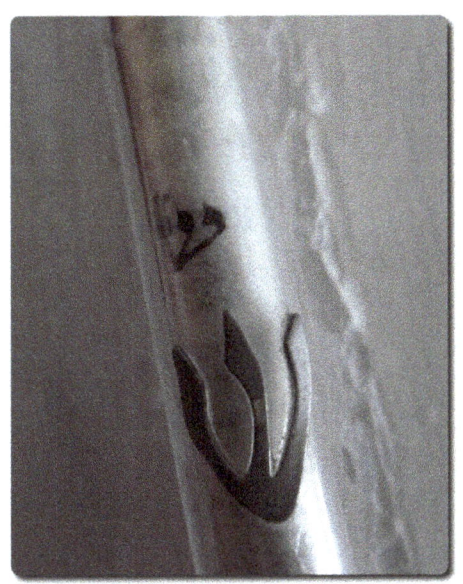

Notice how the top of the Mezuzah is slanted inward.

Appendix C. The Mandala and land defilement

The practice of drawing mandalas is a Hindu tantric ritual that can bring defilement to the land. Experts in occult practices believe that the procedure of drawing or coloring a mandala acts as a portal to bring demonic beings to that place. Mandalas can be used to transmute evil entities into the earth and gives the demons legal right. Tibetan masters are known for the spiritual corruption of land and waterways by use of sand mandalas. Buddhists also employ the use of mandalas to aid in meditation. If your land has been defiled by use of mandalas it needs to be cleansed, healed, and restored. Repent to God for its use by you and your ancestors and ask Him to disconnect you from all the gods and goddesses of Hinduism.

Here are some pictures of mandalas which can be beautiful objects of art.

Appendix D. What to do if after having completed the cleansing and blessing exercises delineated in this book you still sense defilement or an evil presence

After completing the land and home cleansing and blessing ceremony sometimes, though rarely, home owners or tenants continue to feel an evil presence in their home. What is the cause? This happens usually because something exists in the home that should have been removed but remains there because the occupants forgot it was there or because someone in the home is not willing to give it up. Also, allowing an adult to live on your land, in a cottage, house, or apartment without a lease agreement, which defines the area or space they are renting, opens the door for the land you live on to get re-defiled. This re-defilement happens when the guest occupant gets involved in one or more of the sins listed in chapter one.

Another element comes into play and that is the spiritual condition of the man and woman of the home. If they haven't dealt with their own demons, their own issues, they may lack the authority to expel any persistent powers of darkness. That's why I recommend that each have at least one personal ministry session with a skilled freedom minister.

It is important to regularly pray the suggested prayers, "A prayer to pray regularly in your home" and "Another prayer to pray over your family." For married couples I propose that the husband and wife pray these prayers together. My wife and I pray these prayers every night before going to bed.

APPENDIX E. CREATING A HOLY ATMOSPHERE

In addition to praying the above prayers together regularly, my wife, Ruthie, and I pray for each other's needs and other prayer needs of family and friends. Often we spend time thanking and praising God.

Expressing thanks to God for all that He's done helps create clean hearts and pure attitudes and leads to creating an atmosphere of peace and joy within the home. The psalmist impassionedly pleaded, "Oh, that *men* would give **thanks** to the LORD *for* His goodness, And *for* His wonderful works to the children of men" (Psalm 107:8)! The Apostle Paul exhorted the Christians at Ephesus, *Giving thanks always for all things to God the Father in the name of our Lord Jesus Christ* (Ephesians 5:20). And again in 1 Thessalonians 5:18 he wrote, *In everything give thanks; for this is the will of God in Christ Jesus for you.* He makes it clear that giving thanks to God is God's will. And again in Philippians 4:6, *Be anxious for nothing, but in everything by prayer and supplication, with thanksgiving let your requests be made known to God.* The blessing we receive by giving thanks is expressed in the next verse which reads, *And the peace of God, which surpasses all understanding, will guard your hearts and minds through Christ Jesus* (Phil. 4:7). God promises that instead of experiencing anxiety we will enjoy the peace of God. Thanksgiving creates peace and we want peace to not only reside in our hearts but to permeate the spiritual climate of our homes. Ann Voskamp, in her book *One Thousand Gifts*, recommends that we list a thousand things to be thankful for. It may take several months but I have found this exercise to be quite beneficial and uplifting.

Thanksgiving is not an option for us to choose once in a while if we feel like it or when everything is going well. Thanksgiving is a command. In my Bible I find 109 references to this form of worship. And amazingly, when we obey, even when we don't feel like giving thanks, our heart begins to change and after a while, after expressing thanks out of sheer obedience, we usually feel like giving thanks.

Praising God also helps purify the home environment. Notice the Psalmist's words in Psalm 71:8, *Let my mouth be filled with Your praise and with Your glory all the day.* He wanted to praise God throughout the day. Praise invites the Presence of God. Some people find it helpful to play soft worship music in every room of their home 24/7, but whatever you do, make sure to offer praises to Almighty God regularly. Praise truly changes our home environment, but even if we received no benefits from praise, God is worthy to be praised.

Another activity that helps consecrate the ambiance of the home is the reading of the Bible out loud. When Joshua was getting ready to lead the Children of Israel into the Promised Land he no doubt experienced anxiety regarding this monumental task. God spoke to him saying,

> *This Book of the Law shall not depart from your mouth, but you shall meditate in it day and night, that you may observe to do according to all that is written in it. For then you will make your way prosperous, and then you will have good success (Joshua 1:8).*

We usually think of Biblical meditation as a quiet exercise of the heart. However, the Hebrew word, "*wahagita,*" translated as "meditate" in this verse means to imagine, mourn, mutter, roar, speak, talk, utter, groan, ruminate, and roll over in the mind. Notice that much of it has to do with what comes out our mouth and God told Joshua to not let it depart from his mouth. Reading the word silently is good but reading and meditating on it out loud is even better.

In Deuteronomy 6:4-8 we read,

> *Hear, O Israel: The LORD our God, the LORD is one!* [5] *You shall love the LORD your God with all your heart, with all your soul, and with all your strength.*[6] *"And these words which I command you today shall be in your heart.* [7] *You shall teach them diligently to your children, and shall talk of them when you sit in your house, when you walk by the way, when you lie down, and when you rise up.* [8] *You shall bind them as a sign on your hand, and they shall be as frontlets between your eyes.*

God wants the speaking of His Word to be central in the lives of His people and the spoken Word can powerfully change the dynamics of the home, especially when those words flow from a pure heart.

Ruthie and I regularly read three chapters of the Bible in the evening and discuss its contents. I believe the vibration of the spoken words somehow gradually gets imprinted into the physical structure of the home itself making it holy and glorifying to God. Can I prove this? Only experientially. As I go into homes or other buildings where the Word of God is frequently spoken I can sense the Presence of the Lord. The glory of God seems to permeate the walls, ceiling, and furniture.

Appendix F. Communion Service to Cleanse the Land

Here is a suggested order of service for communion. You may use this one or another, but please don't violate your local church's protocol regarding Holy Communion. Some churches believe that communion is to be celebrated only as a church-wide event. Others insist that only the priest or the pastor may officiate. If this is the case, ask the priest or the pastor to attend the land and house cleansing and blessing ceremony and to lead the communion service. Some churches may balk at the idea of burying the remaining elements so don't cause division by insisting the communion be celebrated in a certain way. God has called us to live in peace and to submit to those in authority over us.

However, I believe the communion service is important and vital in cleansing the land. In the Old Testament the blood of bulls, goats, and sheep was used to make atonement for sins. In the New Testament era the blood of Jesus, that final sacrifice, was shed to provide forgiveness of sins. Every time we participate in The Lord's Supper, we make a vivid statement to the kingdom of darkness that Jesus defeated them through His broken body, His shed blood, and His resurrection. The Bible is quite clear that without the shedding of blood there is no remission of sins. In cleansing the land, sin, not demons, is the main issue because it is sin that defiles the land. And sin has been dealt with at the cross through the shedding of Jesus' blood.

INTRODUCTORY COMMUNION PRAYER *(leader prays):*
Let us pray,

> *God, our Father in heaven, we bow in Your presence and thank You for not sparing Your only Son.*
>
> *We know that You, our Lord Jesus Christ, are risen from the dead. You are alive and here with us. Please now direct your angels to gather all the defilement from this land. Bind and banish Satan and his minions to their appropriate place.*
>
> *Let the Body and Blood of our Lord heal all the wounds inflicted on this land by the evil acts of those who have walked this land and by evil spirits who were empowered to dwell here.*
>
> *Father, we come as stumbling children who neither understand nor know how to pray. Send your Holy Spirit to intercede for us.*
>
> *We ask this in the name of our Lord Jesus Christ, Amen.*

READING *(ask for a volunteer to read):*

John 14:1-6

"Do not let your hearts be troubled. You believe in God; believe also in me.

[2] *My Father's house has many rooms; if that were not*

so, would I have told you that I am going there to prepare a place for you?

³ And if I go and prepare a place for you, I will come back and take you to be with me that you also may be where I am.

⁴ You know the way to the place where I am going."

⁵ Thomas said to him, "Lord, we don't know where you are going, so how can we know the way?"

⁶ Jesus answered, "I am the way and the truth and the life. No one comes to the Father except through me."

THE LORD'S PRAYER *(group prayer)*

Our Father, who art in heaven,
   hallowed be thy Name,
   thy kingdom come,
   thy will be done,
     on earth as it is in heaven.
Give us this day our daily bread.
And forgive us our trespasses,
   as we forgive those
     who trespass against us.
And lead us not into temptation,
   but deliver us from evil,
For thine is the kingdom,
   and the power, and the glory,
   for ever and ever. Amen.

CONFESSION OF SIN

Leader: We confess that we and those who have dwelt on this land have sinned before You

All: Lord, have mercy

Leader: We confess that we and those who have dwelt on this land have failed to forgive one another

All: Lord, have mercy

Leader: We confess that we and those who have dwelt on this land have failed to forgive our ancestors.

All: Lord, have mercy

A Moment of Silent Prayer to Confess Our Sins Against God and Our Neighbor

COMMUNION *(leader prays):*

Almighty God, we stop to remember the suffering and sacrifice of our Lord Jesus Christ on the cross of Calvary. We remember His shed blood, His death, resurrection, and ascension. Sanctify and bless these elements by Your Holy Spirit to be for Your children the Body and Blood of Your Son. We ask this in the name of the Lord Jesus Christ of Nazareth. Amen.

(leader distributes the bread and says): On that night in the upper room, our Lord and Savior Jesus Christ took bread, and after giving thanks, He broke it and gave it to His disciples, and said, "Take eat: This is my Body, which is given for you. do this in remembrance of me."

(leader distributes the cup and says): After supper Jesus took the cup of wine, and after giving thanks, He gave it to them and said, "All of you drink of it. This is my blood of the new covenant, which is shed for you and for many for the forgiveness of sins."

PRAYER AFTER COMMUNION

(leader prays): Remember Your servants who dwell on this land, O Lord, according to the favor that You bear unto your people, and grant that increasing in knowledge and love of You, they may go from strength to strength and attain to the fullness of joy that You purpose for them. Expectantly awaiting our own resurrection, we celebrate also the future transfiguration of the whole created order in harmony and beauty. Lord You have made the world for joy and you lead souls from the depth of sin to holiness. Grant to the occupants of this land a new life in the unchanging light of the Lamb of God, who lives and reigns with You, and the Holy Spirit now and forever. Amen.

Dig a hole and bury the leftover bread and wine and cover the elements with dirt. This action will leave an imprint of God's presence on the land. Burying the communion elements is not foreign to Christian religious groups around the world. In Anglican tradition for one, the priest will often pour the leftover blessed wine onto the earth after the church service.

Blessing by the Team Leader

May God the Father Almighty continue to heal this land that it may be used for His glory. We ask this blessing in the name of the Father, and of the Son, and of the Holy Spirit.

All: Amen.

Appendix G. Some Uses of Salt in the Scriptures

In the Bible salt was used to purify. Here is an example from the life of Elisha,

> *Then the men of the city said to Elisha, "Please notice, the situation of this city is pleasant, as my lord sees; but the water is bad, and the ground barren." And he said, "Bring me a new bowl, and put **salt** in it." So they brought it to him. Then he went out to the source of the water, and cast in the **salt** there, and said, "Thus says the* LORD: *'I have healed this water; from it there shall be no more death or barrenness.'" So the water remains healed to this day, according to the word of Elisha which he spoke (2 Kings 2:19-22, emphasis added).*

In this passage we see that salt was used as a vehicle for healing the water and land.

In addition, Ezekiel mentions salt in connection to cleansing the altar.

> *When you have finished cleansing it, you shall offer a young bull without blemish, and a ram from the flock*

> *without blemish. When you offer them before the LORD, the priests shall throw **salt** on them, and they will offer them up as a burnt offering to the LORD (Ezekiel 43:23-24, emphasis added).*

The Lord instructed Moses to use salt in purifying the incense for the altar of incense.

> *And the LORD said to Moses: "Take sweet spices, stacte and onycha and galbanum, and pure frankincense with these sweet spices; there shall be equal amounts of each. You shall make of these an incense, a compound according to the art of the perfumer, **salted**, pure, and holy (Exodus 30:34-35, emphasis added).*

God also commanded the Old Testament believers to offer their grain offerings with salt.

> *And every offering of your grain offering you shall season with salt; you shall not allow the salt of the covenant of your God to be lacking from your grain offering. With all your offerings you shall offer salt (Leviticus 2:13).*

Salt referred to the covenant the Israelites had with God. When Elisha asked for salt, he was reminding them of the covenant they had with God and because they were in a covenant relationship with the LORD He would remove the curse upon the water and land.

On the other hand, sometimes invading armies would sow the land with large amounts of salt to make the land barren so salt could be used as a symbol of judgment. In Judges 9:45 we read,

> *So Abimelech fought against the city all that day; he took the city and killed the people who were in it; and he demolished the city and sowed it with salt.*

When Elisha used salt he was judging what the enemy was doing to oppress this city.

Salt was normally used for positive purposes such as purifying, flavoring and preserving. Therefore, I believe it is good, right and appropriate to use blessed salt as an instrument in cleansing the land.

Preparing the Salt

It is easy to prepare the salt. First, pour some salt into a small bowl. Estimate approximately how much salt you will need based on the size of the property. You will use only a tiny pinch at a time because you don't want to sterilize the land. Place your hands over the bowl and say something like this,

> *In Jesus' Name I command all evil to leave this salt down to even the atomic and subatomic level. Lord, I ask You to bless this salt. Sanctify it and let Your anointing rest upon each granule. I speak blessings over this salt, in Jesus' Name, Amen.*

I recommend that the prayer ministers bless the salt before arriving at the scene in order to save time at the ministry site.

Appendix H. Trauma Bonds to Land

We have found that when a person is severely traumatized on a piece of land they develop a trauma bond to that land. The trauma bond connects them to that land in an unhealthy way, making it more difficult to heal from the traumatic event. They also form an ungodly link to all others who were traumatized on that same property. A soul tie is a direct link to others that is formed through sex outside of marriage, control, abuse, and ungodly covenants. A soul tie allows the other person's stuff to flow to you and your issues to them. Similarly, a trauma bond establishes an indirect link between you and others that were traumatized on that same tract of land. When we break the trauma bonds to the land we are trusting God to free all people who have been bonded to the land in an ungodly way.

In the movie, *Forest Gump*, there is a scene where Forest and Ginny go to visit the house where she grew up, a place where she suffered horrific trauma. When Ginny sees the house her countenance changes. She reaches down and in a rage proceeds to throw rocks at the house, one after another, until she runs out of steam and out of rocks and falls down crying. Then Forest makes the comment, "Sometimes there's just not enough rocks." That scene aptly describes a person who received trauma on a property and has developed a trauma bond to that land.

Appendix I. Preparing the Anointing Oil

As with the salt, it is easy to bless oil. Take olive oil and pour it into a small container, one that is the appropriate size for the land you have in mind. It doesn't matter if you use organic extra pure virgin oil or a less expensive variety of olive oil. Place your hands over the oil and say,

> *In Jesus' Name, I command all evil to leave this oil even down to the molecular, atomic, and subatomic level. I decree and declare this oil is sanctified, set apart for Yahweh's holy use. Lord, let Your anointing rest upon this oil and bless it, in Jesus' Name, Amen.*

I recommend that the prayer ministers bless the oil before arriving at the scene in order to save time at the ministry site.

The Biblical Basis for the Use of Oil

Oil was used to consecrate the Old Testament tabernacle and its furnishings. In Exodus 40:9 we read,

> *And you shall take the anointing oil, and anoint the tabernacle and all that is in it; and you shall hallow it and all its utensils, and it shall be holy.*

In Numbers 7:1 we are told,

> *Now it came to pass, when Moses had finished setting up the tabernacle, that he anointed it and consecrated it and all its furnishings, and the altar and all its utensils; so he anointed them and consecrated them.*

Dictionary.com defines the verb "to consecrate" as, "to make or declare sacred; set apart or dedicate to the service of a deity." Therefore, when we anoint our land with oil we can say that we are dedicating it to the service of Almighty God.

Oil was also used in conjunction with prayers for healing. In James 5:14 we read,

> *Is anyone among you sick? Let him call for the elders of the church, and let them pray over him, anointing him with oil in the name of the Lord.*

In Mark 6:12-13 we discover that when Jesus sent the twelve disciples out they used oil when praying for the sick.

> *So they went out and preached that people would repent. And they cast out many demons, and anointed with oil many who were sick, and healed them.*

The anointing can rest upon inanimate objects, as can be seen in the New Testament when the anointing transferred to handkerchiefs that could be used as agents of healing. Similarly, the anointing of the Holy Spirit rests upon the blessed anointing oil which can be used of God to heal the land.

Jacob experienced God in a new way when God appeared to him in a dream promising him great and mighty things. The encounter so moved Jacob that he never wanted to forget that pivotal moment in his life. He set up a memorial stone, a monument to God's favor upon him, and then he consecrated it by anointing the stone with oil.

> *Then Jacob rose early in the morning, and took the stone that he had put at his head, set it up as a pillar,*

and poured oil on top of it (Genesis 28:18).

Ancient literature records many instances of sacred stones which were anointed with oil, so it is not some strange thing to anoint our land with oil.

Appendix J. Ley Lines

Homeowners experience frustration after they cleanse and bless their land, only to discover that the defilement, and the bad fruit that comes from that defilement never left. This incomplete cleansing may be the result of failing to deal with a ley line that runs through their property. The presence of a ley line will affect the occupants of a home or office. To illustrate, a lady moved into her new home and immediately suffered from extreme insomnia. A prayer team went to her house and discovered a ley line that ran across her bed. When they broke the ley line she had no problem sleeping.

What is a ley line? Many people refer to them as a grid of earth energies which circles the globe, and connects famous revered sites such as the Borobudur, Indonesia, Batu Caves, Malaysia, Great Wall of China, Stonehenge, and the Egyptian Pyramids. Interestingly, if you look at these and other sacred sites on a map you can see that many of them can be connected by straight lines. In the 19th century on the British Islands many people believed in mystifying "fairy paths," trails connecting certain hilltops in the countryside. It was considered hazardous and ill advised to travel on those paths during certain days because the hiker might come upon a parade of fairies who would become angry for being disturbed by a human.

Ley lines were discovered in modern history by Alfred Watkins in 1921, a respected businessman, who was viewing a map and observed a straight line that ran over hilltops through a variety of ancient interest points. Watkins concluded that these "ley lines," as he named them, were prehistoric trading routes, despite the fact that many ley lines traveled up extremely steep mountainsides. He believed that they were associated with the Greek god Hennes, (or the Roman Mercury or the Norse Woden) who was the god of communication and boundaries, the guide to travelers on unknown paths.

After Watkins death in 1935, speculation regarding the meaning and purpose of ley lines continued. Some believed they were lines of power linking prehistoric sites. Others suggested that ley lines followed lines of cosmic energy in the Earth and could be identified by the use of dowsing rods. In the 1960's some were convinced that ley lines were connected to UFO sightings.

Individuals have advanced various theories regarding the existence and purpose of ley lines but we have come to see that they are simply conduits or channels between two spiritually polluted geographical spots, through which demons travel back and forth. So if an ungodly ley line travels through your land or home you and your family and guests will experience defilement on a regular basis. Arthur Burk with Sapphire Ministries claims that nothing flourishes along an unrighteous ley line. Vegetation, insects, animals, and people do not flourish on an ungodly ley line. Marriages suffer, children suffer, and churches do not do well if positioned on an unrighteous ley line.

I believe that ungodly ley lines are conduits or pathways for demons to travel and communicate. They are typically several inches wide but in some cases prayer ministers have found them to stretch 20 to 25 feet in width depending on how long they have been in existence and the depth of evil at either end. Ley lines may originate on the top of a mountain or hill. Numerous times the Bible references "high places" and God's anger over the idolatrous practices performed there. For example, in 2 Kings 17:11 we read,

> *There they burned incense on the* **high places**, *like the nations whom the* LORD *had carried away before them; and they did wicked things to provoke the* LORD *to anger (emphasis added). And in Numbers 33:52, then you shall drive out all the inhabitants of the land from before you, destroy all their engraved stones, destroy all their molded images, and demolish all their* **high places** *(emphasis added).*

Occultic organizations are drawn to these "high places" or mountaintops or hilltops.

From the high place a ley line will normally go to water, a lake if there is one, or to a valley. Freemasonry lodges and temples usually have a ley line connected as well as drug houses and witchcraft meeting places.

I might add here that not all prayer ministers hold to the same view of ley lines. For example, Paul Cox, with Aslan's Place Ministries, believes that ley lines are contaminated grid lines and are used for evil purposes. He argues that the devil cannot create, he can only pervert or corrupt what God has already created. God created these grid lines to be righteous locations of spiritual movement. Here is a picture illustrating a grid.

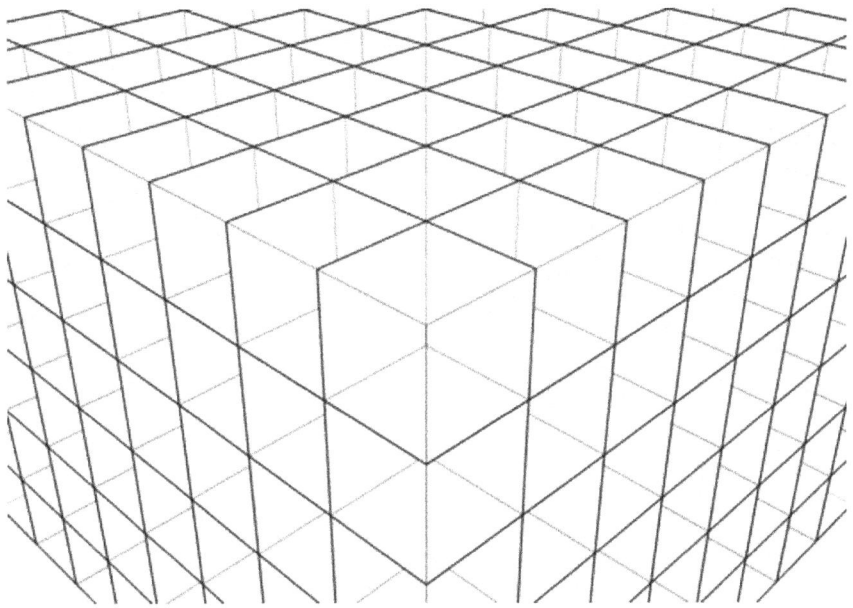

The evil pathway or conduit for the enemy's use lies between the ley lines. Paul Cox doesn't cut the ley line but instead he asks God to remove the contamination of the enemy off the grid line. He says, "The corruption of these lines by the enemy would give permission for the enemy to utilize the lines for evil purposes." I've heard him teach that contaminated ley lines are crooked, while righteous ley lines are straight. My advice is to ask the Lord how He would have you deal with ley lines if you discern their presence.

Some prayer ministers feel called to break the entire ley line at its source. To eliminate the ley line in full may be ideal but, because it often takes a great deal of time, training, effort and commitment so for our purposes, we will focus on breaking or cleansing the ley line at the specific property we are cleansing. So if the ley line begins on a hilltop the demonic travel has to stop when it reaches the cleansed property, like water in a pipe that flows to a closed valve and can't get through.

How to Discern a Ley Line

As the prayer team walks the property line dribbling the anointing oil be sensitive to your human spirit and to the Holy Spirit who indwells all true followers of Christ. If you sense something change, stop and see if anyone else on the prayer team senses something. It is recommended that both men and women serve on the team because often men will sense something while the women don't and vice versa. You may sense a spot of defilement on the land or it may be a ley line. Some prayer ministers make use of an electromagnetic force reader or a compass for confirmation because if these gadgets move when you bring them to a particular spot it could be an indicator of a demonic pathway. This method is not foolproof because there could be movement due to an underground electric cable or iron ore. So when you sense something negative in your spirit as you walk the perimeter make a mental note of where that was on the property. Continue to work your way around, staking the corners and dribbling the anointing oil. If you feel the same thing on the other side of the property you may have the presence of an unrighteous ley line running through the property.

Don't think you have to locate a ley line on every property in order to properly cleanse it. If you don't discern the presence of a ley line don't get hung up on this issue but I mention it here so that you will have some tools in case this situation arises. It could be that to experience complete freedom you must deal with these ley lines but seek the Lord to see what He instructs you to do.

How to Remove or Cleanse a Ley Line

Once you discern a ley line go to it and ask God to identify the major sin(s) that opened the door. Remember, evil spiritual beings are not the big issue. It is sin that human beings committed that gave the devil legal ground to contaminate the land. Ask yourself, "What do I discern in my spirit; what changed?" You may feel pain in your body, greed, lust, anger, heaviness, etc. Ask God what that feeling means. Then confess (agreeing with God) and renounce the sins you discern that were committed on that land.

Ask God to break, shatter, cut off, dissolve, and destroy the evil of this pathway. The owner or tenant says,

> *I ask You Heavenly Father to cleanse the ley lines running through this land. I decree and declare that no highway for demonic spirits can cross this property, in Jesus' Name.*

Ask God to set an angelic guard on the property lines where this ley line ran, to forbid any wicked spirits access through a ley line.

Appendix K. Occultic Paraphernalia in the Home by Greg Solomon

Before I get into this subject I want to share with you why this has become really heavy on my heart. I want to take an approach that is not from a legalistic standpoint.

I go back to the story of Adam and Eve in the garden and the one thing that God told them not to eat from was the tree of the knowledge of good and evil. He intended for them to have Life... and have it abundantly. I believe that God's intention for us is not for us to eat of the tree of the knowledge of good and evil. On the other hand, it says in Hosea 4:6,

"My people perish for their lack of knowledge."

So I feel like it's my duty, having the knowledge of this, to share my heart with you in that and not be legalistic about it, and not be "Is it right or wrong?" I don't want to be the authority in telling you certain things are right and wrong. But what I really want to do is ask you to search your heart and ask the Holy Spirit to search your heart to see and bring all of these things before God.

Now the reason this is heavy on my heart is because I have a past. I didn't always believe that Jesus is Lord. I didn't believe in Jesus. Period. I didn't believe in God for a long time.

It was when I met and formed a relationship with my Heavenly Father that I recognized the point, the blessing of knowing Him and knowing His will for my life. Now when I didn't have a relationship with my Father I was the only authority in my life. I got into some stuff I shouldn't have been into.

I was big into Halloween, I mean that was my favorite holiday. I didn't see anything bad about it. I'm not just talking about wearing a funny outfit. I'm talking about decapitated heads and skulls, skeletons, demons, and ghosts. Anything scary and gory… it was how I decorated.

Then at one point, I noticed every time I did, even after I became a Christian, I would get severely ill at that time of year. At one point I was bedridden with pneumonia and couldn't function. I was self-employed at the time and couldn't work but I was still able to go decorate and celebrate Halloween. Then right after the holiday, I was bedridden for weeks.

So I began to really press in and pray to the Lord… asking for revelation. "Was I really honoring Him by honoring and celebrating these things? Why were these things described as 'detestable' to Him?"

Now I want to be very clear about this part. I didn't feel condemned about this at all. I didn't beat myself up and ask, "How could you do that to yourself?" However, the Holy Spirit convicted my heart in a very simple way… to not want to associate with or honor anything that He would consider detestable.

Now here's the tricky part. The enemy can be deceitful. Some of the most evil things we encounter are cleverly disguised and marketed as harmless games, cartoons, and collectibles. This is what makes these activities so attractive to the youth of our generation.

My hope in sharing this with you is that it will shed some light on what a lot of kids are going through right now. It may upset some people… and if that applies to you, you may want to ask yourself why.

This is exactly why I get into this teaching of what to look for in your home that can provide an opening for the enemy, and how to be aware of what you or your kids are doing.

Demonic Games

The enemy has bombarded the youth of today's culture with a plethora of demonic games. They inspire individuals to plug into the dark side by sending spells and hexes against their opponents. The games may seem harmless because "everybody is doing it," but they provide an opening for evil spirits to defile the home. What good does it do to cleanse and bless the home if the children continue to invite in evil presences through these games? If you allow these games into your home does that mean that God stops loving you or that you lose your salvation? Of course not. But our desire is for you to live in the maximum freedom that God has for you. Therefore, we recommend that the following games be avoided:

Pendulums/Fortune Telling

When a pregnant mother dangles a pendulum over her belly in order to determine the gender of her child she opens the door for physical maladies in her child. Quite often the child will suffer from asthma and other breathing difficulties. It behooves the mother to repent and renounce all such activities.

Charlie, Charlie

Players invoke a Mexican spirit by using two pencils as a pendulum. This is similar to the concept of using a Ouija board, in that the object is to get the spirit to move the pencils at the X/Y axis to answer yes and no questions. This game has become a trend in the youth today, as millions of kids took part in the "Charlie Charlie challenge" across different social media platforms. In May 2015 in St. John's Antigua, students were reported to have been fainting, having seizures, and trying to jump off of the school bus after a group was suspended for playing the game at the school.

Magic 8-ball

A similar concept to the Charlie Charlie game, in which a large 8-ball with variations of YES/NO questions is used in fortune telling. Popularity for the magic 8-ball has decreased in recent years, but has risen in popularity after becoming a mobile app for smart phones and tablets.

> *"Do not turn to mediums or necromancers; do not seek them out, and so make yourselves unclean by them: I am the LORD your God. (Leviticus 19:31 ESV)*

Collectible Card Games (CCG)

Collectible card games have become a staple among the youth, starting in the mid 1990's. While they may appear fun and innocent, there is no denying their occultic influence.

Unfortunately, some churches have resorted to hosting various card game tournaments with the youth, giving ground to the demonic forces and defiling their land in a misguided attempt to connect with the youth of today. Rather than bringing the glory of God to the youth, they are bringing the presence of evil into the church.

Most card games have a similar combat concept... collecting various cards that enable the player to protect, attack, cast spells, enchant, make demonic pacts, and summon demons. Games like 'Magic: the Gathering' focus on the powers of witchcraft, sorcery, and wizards and warlocks... with the goal of the game being to rule over your opponent through forces of darkness.

Magic: The Gathering

Some recent card types include:
- Demonic Pact
- Seeker of 'the Way'
- Anointer of Champions
- Dragon Hunter
- Honored Hierarch
- Haven of the Spirit Dragon
- Shrine of the Forsaken Gods

Japanimation/Anime Games

Anime is a popular genre of eastern animation among the youth and traveling CONS (conventions), dating back to the early 1980's. While the premise of Asian CCG's is similar, it is combined with a much more sophisticated marketing strategy geared towards younger kids - from action cartoons to t-shirts, toys, movies and video games.

Yu-Gi-Oh!

The *movie* and *television* show have much in common with the *Harry Potter* series. Both are grade school boys with magical powers which they use for good. Each has a nemesis in a more popular older kid. Instead of European mythology and witches, Yugi's character is a blend of Asian and Egyptian beliefs, suffused with science fiction and robots.

A sophisticated CCG is the basis for the franchise; the movie gives a better understanding of how the games are played. Each card summons up magical spells or monsters. Each card can be trumped by another if it is well chosen.

Other Similar Shows/Games/Franchises

Pokemon

Although the message behind the series is said to teach principles of love and compassion, the show and games feature a battle of cute pet-like monsters. The CCG also includes cards for channeling spirits, telepathy, demonic possession, conjuring demons, and casting spells to defeat/kill your opponent. In chapter three of his book, *Buying & Selling the Souls of Our Children*, the late dearly loved John Paul Jackson made some poignant comments about the demonic influence of certain popular games.

"It was only a stone idol bought on a vacation while in India. The people who bought it weren't Hindu. To them, it was merely exotic art. However, after placing the statue in their home, strange things began to happen. They began having disturbing dreams. Their beloved cat mysteriously died. A feeling of depression and fear permeated the house. It wasn't long before they both became ill."

"When a discerning friend identified the source of trouble—the Indian artifact—the couple quickly disposed of it and repented for bringing it into their home. Finally, they were delivered from the demonic attack that wreaked havoc in their lives."

"While the couple did not worship the stone artifact, dark spirits and a dark philosophy were attached to it. Furthermore, the stone idol opened doors for the demonic realm to harass them. In a similar way, demonic attacks come from a door we open, knowingly or unknowingly. Simply bringing a pagan object into your home can have sinister results."

"While many Christians would not allow their children to bring a pentagram or voodoo doll into their homes, they have unknowingly opened a door to the demonic. They have done this simply by allowing their children to play games that are pagan, and that employ principles practiced in occult worship. It's my belief that Pokémon, and games that bear resemblance to it, open demonic doors that can unleash spiritual attacks on the unsuspecting, as well as on those who embrace the dark side." (John Paul Jackson, *Buying & Selling the Souls of Our Children*, Copyright © 2000, Published by Streams Publications, pp, 17-18)

DRAGON BALL Z

Features witches and wizards, who are experts in the art of magic (and possibly the art of fortune-telling and divination), some are even capable of creating other beings through magic, reviving the dead, and/or summoning spirits or demons to serve them.

Computer/Console Games

MMORPG | Massive Multiplayer Online Role Playing Games

Multiplayer RPG's have become a global sensation. In November 2013, an estimated count of 1.2 billion users playing games, with over 700 million gamers playing online at any given part of the day.

The theme of the most popular games is the fantasy combat games, similar to the premise of Magic: The Gathering and other games featuring witchcraft and wizardry. World of Warcraft favors heavily to the demonic, with titles "The Demon Soul" and "Legion."

World of Warcraft (books & games)

- Day of the Dragon
- Lord of the Clans
- The Last Guardian
- Of Blood and Honor
- The Well of Eternity
- The Demon Soul
- The Sundering
- World of Warcraft: Legion
- Tides of Darkness
- Beyond the Dark Portal

The Elder Scrolls Series

This series is again similar to the World of Warcraft franchise, featuring similar mystical creatures of witchcraft and wizardry.

- Arena

- Daggerfall
- Morrowind
- Oblivion
- Sky Rim

This does not represent an exhaustive list by any means. Seeing as the majority of these titles share a similar premise, many lesser known similar titles are available, including expansion packs for the existing titles. This list focuses on the more popular games in this era. While online gaming continues to grow in numbers, companies are strategically moving to mobile gaming platforms to gain more subscribers.

> *When you come into the land that the Lord your God is giving you, you shall not learn to follow the abominable practices of those nations. There shall not be found among you anyone who burns his son or his daughter as an offering, anyone who practices divination or tells fortunes or interprets omens, or a sorcerer or a charmer or a medium or a necromancer or one who inquires of the dead, for whoever does these things is an abomination to the Lord. And because of these abominations the Lord your God is driving them out before you. Deuteronomy 18:9-12 (ESV).*

Appendix L. Blessing Land

Some scientists point out that matter and nature absorbs sound and they are working on ways to retrieve the sounds from inanimate objects. We know that playing classical music helps plants to grow. Birds chirping in a tree help that tree to be more healthy. In a similar way, matter records the sound of the human voice. When Jesus entered the city of Jerusalem on that first Palm Sunday the people gave praise to Him. The religious leaders complained and told Jesus to rebuke His disciples. The story is recorded in Luke 19:37-40,

> *Then, as He was now drawing near the descent of the Mount of Olives, the whole multitude of the disciples began to rejoice and praise God with a loud voice for all the mighty works they had seen, [38] saying: "'Blessed is the King who comes in the name of the LORD!' Peace in heaven and glory in the highest!" And some of the Pharisees called to Him from the crowd, "Teacher, rebuke Your disciples. But He answered and said to them, "I tell you that if these should keep silent, the stones would immediately cry out."*

Could it be that the rocks had recorded the sound of praise? Jesus said that they would have cried out if the crowds kept silent.

I believe we can influence the land by the words of our mouth. Otherwise, why would God lead the people to bless the land in Jeremiah 31:23?

> *Thus says the LORD of hosts, the God of Israel: "They shall again use this speech in the land of Judah and in its cities, when I bring back captivity: 'The LORD bless you, O home of justice, and mountain of holiness!'*

Appendix M. Ungodly Portals

A spiritual portal is an unseen door, gate, or entrance that connects two places through time and space, and even dimensions or other realities. Sometimes mirrors can become an ungodly portal for unwelcomed spiritual guests. Children often like to play the game called Bloody Mary. They repeatedly look in the mirror and chant, "Bloody Mary" and in this manner they are able to conjure up a demon. I strongly recommend that you not let your children play this "innocent" game.

Appendix N. Dream Catchers

The Dream Catcher is a handmade object commonly found in Native American cultures. It consists of a woven net or web that has certain decorations, such as beads, shells, gemstones, leather, feathers and other such things. These adornments are usually items found in nature. The Dream Catcher is typically hung in a bedroom, above a bed, or sometimes above a door. The belief is that happy, positive dreams will pass through the net, while the negative dreams or nightmares will become ensnared, so the dreamer has only optimistic dreams. On the other hand, some believe that the negative dreams pass through the hole in the center of the Dream Catcher, while the good dreams are trapped, and thus become a part of that person's destiny.

So what's so wrong with a Dream Catcher? Even though these pieces of art can be attractive aesthetically, and even though they are popular, my problem with them is twofold.

First, they are based on superstition and a pagan belief system. Second, I can usually sense the presence of a demon on them when I find them in the home of a Christian. If you want to be free, my recommendation is to get rid of them. Here are some pictures of typical dreams catchers.

Summary

By applying the above truths you will enjoy the benefits of a cleansed and blessed land and home. Once you remove the evil by repentance and prayer you will experience more of the peace of God. But don't look at this procedure as a quick fix, a one-time deal. Think of it as a process of walking in righteousness and holy living. Seek the Lord daily in praise and worship and through meditating on the Word of God. Make it your aim to walk according to your God-ordained destiny and your home and land will ever-increasingly reflect the glory of God. Your land and home will testify to the goodness of Almighty God.

www.ingramcontent.com/pod-product-compliance
Lightning Source LLC
LaVergne TN
LVHW010317070426
835507LV00026B/3434